SPLIT

SOULS IN TRANSITION

BY

ALFRED HARRELL

S
P
L
I
T

Published by: Listen Black Media, LLC
Text Design by: Tyrrell Harrell
Cover Design by: Tyrrell Harrell

A record for this book is available from the Library of Congress Cataloging-in-Publication Data

Print ISBN: 978-1-962799-01-0
Digital ISBN: 978-1-962799-02-7

Distributed by:
Ingram Spark
1246 Heil Quaker Blvd
La Vergne, TN 37086

Alfred Harrell

SPLIT

Souls in Transition

I decided that it was not wisdom that enabled poets to write their poetry, but a kind of instinct or inspiration, such as you find in seers and prophets who deliver all their sublime messages without knowing in the least what they mean.

-Socrates

Author's Note

December 25, 2021 was the first Christmas day together for me and Karen. This was one of very few Christmas days within the past several years I had actually taken off work from any job of mine. This in itself, one might think, should have created certain measures of peace in my soul however it did not. As our morning progressed I became restless and an overwhelming urge to turn on my laptop and begin working on this book came over me.

Peace struggled to find its way in my inner being; my soul. One thing that hindered my peace from arriving was knowing that it would be the first Christmas I did not spend with my little grandkids because of unresolved issues with their parents as well as my Christmas Eve work schedule. I did, however, receive a very brief phone call from my 4 year old grandson thanking me for his new kid-sized camera. A further hindrance to embracing personal peace was my failure to truly honor and display my appreciation for the amazing woman, Karen, with whom I was spending this day of relaxation with.

Some time, I think, before 9 AM, I caved in to that burning desire to write. Along with that came unplanned moments of prayer as a mentally padlocked door of memories, good and bad, began to flood my mind. Sometimes like a refreshing shower and at other moments, like a nightmare movie reel stories with myself, with others and life events associated with our collective human experience.

The section, SEVEN Black Relationships Personified, is the culmination of some writings from years past as well as words that started finding their way out of my mental prison on December 25, 2021. A day I will remember as the 25th of December.

~ Alfred Harrell

Foreword

by Karen A. Sims, M. Ed.

Courage, power and respect are words that are often overused and at the same time misunderstood by many. The misunderstanding of these words is often shown in the little lives lived by those who hold extraordinary talent and immeasurable favor, but refuse to share their talents to change the world. You will not see evidence of any shirking in this writing. Mr. Alfred Harrell is bold in his imagery and direct in his storytelling. The deepest family secrets are being revealed in hopes to incite the riot needed to encourage change and healing. You see his courage as he speaks of his personal accounts of trauma, discovery, self-rediscovery and even the rebirthing of himself into true manhood.

Luke 12:48 (KJV) "To whom much is given, much is required" is a biblical passage that we have heard so often we may have forgotten the actual meaning behind the words. We all have gifts to share. I am pleased that the time has come for Mr. Harrell to share these words and gifts with you all. You will travel to the darkest tunnels and emerge into some of the sun-shiniest parts of his life, but not without being changed within your very core. As you embark on this poetic journey, I challenge you to take the barriers off of yourself and be immersed in the many facets that are included in this beautiful tribute and awesome form of literary wonder. Take this journey to places that are often only kept in the recesses of our minds or even places that we could never really imagine. Those "off-limits" memories. Mr. Harrell's words will be your guide during this literary journey.

I hesitate to tell you to be prepared for a whirlwind because ingesting this work will manifest a little bit differently in each mind. I will encourage you to stay open, reflect on each written word and feel the stories and memories that have been shared in these pages.

As an author, poet, and inspirational speaker it brings me great joy to delve into real soulful writing that has the power to move me at my core. Souls in Transition has done just that. Words about my personal impact on Mr. Harrell's heart condition have created a soothing melody to this love rhythm that we continue to unfold. Real love reveals and real love heals.

Matthew 24:13 (NKJV) "But he who endures to the end shall be saved." Alfred, I share my respect, love and pride that you are making it til the end. Cheers to a wonderful journey ahead.

Mental Health Matters. Black Lives Matter. Healing Hearts Matter.

May you rediscover the best that a healing heart can receive as you read through these pages.

Miracles & Blessings to All -- Karen A. Sims, M.E

South Elm Street at West McGee Street-Invisible
Greensboro, NC

Dressed in fatigues like he once wore upon a foreign jungle battlefield he feeds himself from a garbage can near the railroad tracks

Nobody sees him but the poet and death waiting in the shadows of the sun to claim his haunted soul

His battle scars are long healed however he still bleeds each times he closes his eyes to sleep, he slips into seemingly never ending nightmares

Nobody speaks to him but the poet and death who whispers to him like a cool breeze blowing

Another train roars by him

He answers deaths whisper

And

Leaps

Hemorrhage

We are bleeding from the inside out, we have been bleeding and still are bleeding from the time we first set foot upon the shores of this country named the United States of America as indentured servants, slaves and free people with our freedom being defined generationally by the religious and ruling powers of this nation.

We are bleeding from the inside out, we have been bleeding and still are from invisible wounds associated with generational trauma birthed in our cultural history, family history, community violence and the social injustices we suffer often now played out upon unsociable social media platforms.

We are bleeding out, our words are bleeding out like Jesus Christ bled blood filled tears, our words are bleeding out like thunder.

We are bleeding out!

Praying Woman (Revised)

Daily she survives the doctrinal changes of Christianity
Because she is not a survivor, she is an overcomer
Daily she survives Christianity's periodic loss of humanity
Because she is the human manifestation of Christ's greatest two commands
Daily she sits upon the edge of her bed praying like a person with nothing to lose
Because she knows that life and death is in the power of the tongue
Daily she prays for people spiritually broken by wolves in sheep's clothing
Because she has personally experienced the healing power of Christ's Holy Spirit
Daily she prays for the abused child, the abused husband, the abused wife

She remembers she used to be one
She remembers when she touched His spiritual garment
She remembers His power healing her bleeding heart

Daily she prays that more people find the peace she's found
Because the peace of God surpasses, is greater than any human ideology
Daily she soaks the wounds of her prayers in His love
Because Christ, once wounded, transfers her prayers into reality
Daily she
She prays

Photo by Askar Abayev

Talking Hands

Bent twisted knuckles knotted from the tips of her fingers to the palms of her hands
Told more stories

Told more stories than library books
The life lines of her hands spoke volumes with their silent tongues

Long curved life lines ran from her wrists like the long fields of white cotton
Picked by her and countless generations before her

Her hands held stories of babies born and children buried before their time
Her hands held the memories the bloody history of men and women murdered
For just being Black

Her hands held history written in their leather like skin
Soles human shoes of freedoms gained

Her hands told tales of sacrifice and salvation stolen from hells fire born under a Southern sun
Her hands spoke with symbols of falling leaves
When she positioned them across a full moon's face

Her hands bore the joys and scars of changing seasons

Spring to summer
Summer to fall
Fall to winter
Winter

Winter finally silenced her talking hands

The Evolutions Of Seven

First of Seven

As far as I can remember pivotal moments in my life happened over coincidental seven year time spans or at times that involved the numeral seven. For instance, I was allowed to attend my first high school sporting event around the age of 13 which was about 7 seven years from when I received and read my first comic book. While what I just shared may seem trivial or normal in some aspects to you, they were life-changers for me as a child who was mentally and physically shut off from influences outside the home other than attending school. Thankfully, my mother found the courage to step in and interfere with the matriarch of our house that was rarely a home, my grandmother's dysfunctional and at times abusive form of nurturing, which I believe she learned in her childhood. She, my grandmother, was born either during or shortly after her parents became freed Black slaves according to one of the few stories she shared during my childhood. Her actual birthday to the best of my knowledge isn't known because records of Negro birth weren't recorded outside of perhaps a family Bible in the county of her birth, Hyde County, North Carolina.

In the poems associated with this segment I pay homage to her troubled life. I also pay tribute to my mother and the greatest male influencer I had during those years, though I wouldn't see him as such until after his death, my stepfather Howard Corey aka Howard Corey.

Second of Seven
MENTORS FOR NEW PERSPECTIVES

Now back to how my mothers challenge to her authority altered my life course as a youth. At approximately the age 13, I would be allowed to learn the game of tennis under the tutelage of Willy Satchel, go on to be taught Karate by Willie O'neal and then find the courage to write my first poem, "I Am," because of my school teacher George Wahabs. Unlike some young people who enter high school with at least an inkling of what they want to do after graduating, I discovered what I wanted to possibly do after high school, when a US Navy recruiter named Hip Holcomb showed up at our small town school talking about the opportunities and advantages of joining the Navy over what the other branches of the United States military offered. Man, I was hooked! I convinced my mother that that was what I wanted to do upon graduation and so she signed the papers for me to join the Navy by means of what was known, back then, as the Navy's Early Enlistment Program because I was only 17 years old. Again the number reared its head.

Third of Seven
CHANGE OF DIRECTION-Personal Choice

Then Bam! As best that I can remember, sometime in 1978, I was convinced by a schoolmate to begin a study of the Bible with Jehovah's Witnesses, whose doctrine of political neutrality, which I would later learn, was totally contrary to my heart's desire and plans of starting a naval career. The young guys who studied the Bible with me by means of the Watchtower's Bible Tract literature also provided me with the casual type of friendship that home life and the limited extra curricular my mother allowed me to participate in during my early teens didn't. This association which created a new kind of personal, mental peace eventually nullified my desire to become a sailor, naval aviator or submariner; I mentioned all three naval options because my ASVAB (Armed Services Aptitude Battery) test scores qualified me for all three areas of work in the NAVY. In the end, Jehovah's Witnesses interpretation of the Bible won out and led me to ask the United States Department of Navy to release me from my sworn oath of service which it did as a conscientious objector in the spring of 1980.

Less than three years later the young men who befriended me moved away from my hometown and the Kingdom Hall (what places of worship for Jehovah's Witnesses are known as0. With them went the friendship I developed with them. That type of friendship would eventually be replaced by other young men and some older ones when I moved to live with my mother and stepfather in Windsor, North Carolina. However, none of these changes associated with the personal spiritual safety net I had discovered provided mental comfort or the peace I truly needed nor the lasting friendships not attached to an "if you act this way or that way then we can be friends" clause.

In hindsight, none of those life changes provided lasting relief or healing from my invisible wounds of living in a mentally and emotionally abusive home for myself, and a physically abusive home for others. None of these changes killed my regret of not honoring my prior naval contract of service or fully suppressed my desire of expressing myself freely through writing. The latter, writing poetry, is occasionally done through censoring my words so they would not violate the doctrines of my conservative, Christian faith.

The marital aspect and family life rooted in conservative, Christian ideology and its interpretation of biblical text slowly became a possible pathway to a mentally, spiritually and emotionally healthy family like I had never experienced. And the friendships associated with it appealed to me because of my encounters with other married people of my adopted faith. However, with Jehovah's Witnesses like some Christian churches, personal intimacy, even a simple hug or kiss upon the cheeks, was frowned upon during dating for fear such contact would violate teachings of sexual abstinence based on selected scriptures written to certain first century Christian churches such as the church at Corinth.

So in the year 1984 I would date and then get married in accord with religious guidelines of Jehovah's Witnesses. I would remain in the marital home for the next 21 years. Over that time I would become the dad to two amazing sons and a husband to a wife who supported the leadership of our family without intimate knowledge of who I truly was or my deeply submerged "why's" for getting up each day. Yes! All the while almost every 7 years during my marriage I pushed back, suppressed almost any desire that threatened my so-called perfect Christian image or Christian family image.

Fourth of Seven
THE BREAK UPS

During my childhood, I inadvertently developed the mental prowess to exist in painful or uncomfortable relationships and situations even to the point of unintentionally suppressing memories, good and bad, in order to love or be loved, to accept or be accepted by others. Periodically my suppressed painful memories would manifest themselves in me as seasons of depression, bouts of verbal anger for no specified reasons and night sweats. I arrived at my final tipping point around the twenty-first year of my marriage when I reached out for spiritual guidance from elders in my local Kingdom Hall located in Jamestown, North Carolina. I was basically told to read, pray and search for possible solutions to what I was dealing with within one of the Watchtower's society' publications written and printed by the governing body of Jehovah's Witnesses.

My biblical research for peace and resolution for my internal conflicts discovered fractures, fissures and misleading information about my chosen form of Christian worship. While I realize that all religious leaders, Christian or otherwise, are flawed in their teaching because we're all imperfect, what bothered me the most and still bothers me is when said leaders choose to not acknowledge publicly or privately to errors contained within their doctrines.

Let the following sink in!

The poisons of control and manipulations served by religious and political leadership or influencers are more easily ingested and digested when hidden in one's favorite dish or dishes.

Like one of Christianity's favorite apostles, the apostle Paul formerly known as Saul of Tarsus, my favorite dishes was my hunger and thirst for God through the biblical text as well as a heart of service for others. The apostle Paul, before being chosen directly by Jesus Christ to be an apostle to the nations, allowed his doctrinal upbringing and knowledge of the code of Law to lead him to hate and hunt down the messengers of the gospel, good news, preached and taught by Jesus Christ. Jesus Christ, the very of whom ancient Hebrew prophets and angels sang about at his birth and God himself referred as his beloved son, affirming this at his baptism by his first cousin, the prophet known as John the Baptist.

Sadly Jehovah's Witnesses, like some other Christian denominations and churches, intentionally or unintentionally focus upon what's wrong with us, our human existence, and our sinfulness. Yeah! Sinfulness of sin which by its most basic definition means missing the mark of perfection nothing more, nothing less. In order to lead and teach people methods of maintaining a spiritually healthy relationship with the Divine, God, I've discovered highlighting the love of God in all of its forms from the rising of the sun to the smile of a newborn's face as methods of drawing us closer to God personally and communally attracts more people to the gospel of the New Testament.

Why didn't I also pursue help from some type of mental health professional? My previous poor experiences with mental health professionals had established great distrust because those that I had received counseling from either offered medications or medications and counseling without conversations where I could share, in depth, the truly painful memories that occasionally surfaced in one form or another.

On this journey I also discovered the value of seeking out mental health counseling and how it adds balance to my ongoing life walk. Let us remember Jesus Christ not only healed individuals physically, he also taught them how to cope mentally as indicated by one of his greatest messages known by many Christians and others as the Sermon on the Mount. So in 2019 I tried counseling for a short while again. Counseling that didn't push some form of drug therapy.

That therapy led to me writing my short collection of healing poems: We Are One Little Boy Lost. That collection of poetry is available on Blurb.com.

Fifth of Seven
THE MAKEUP

Now in the year 2021, another time of seven seems to have appeared in the middle of the Covid-19. I'm finally able to, at the age of 59, embrace without regret, my life's journey, my spiritual journey and being in a fairly free flowing relationship with a woman whose life journey has equipped her to love a man like me.

I'm feeding regularly on a balanced mental diet of spiritual and secular personal growth information and I've reconnected with an earthly spiritual home, or in church vernacular, church home where love of God and service to others by means of one's gifts or talents are more important than religious rules or regulations based upon biblical interpretations.

I invite you to listen to my very first podcast episode "Preconditioned To Fail" published September 3, 2018 on my podcast, Life Is About More Than Living. It covers parts of my story not shared here.

Tribute Poems

Mrs. Francis' Story

This poem is my interpretation of my maternal grandmother's life.

Planting foot in front of foot she traveled under the folds of the morning sun's shadow
To the seafood processing plant planted by the Pungo River bank

Silent was each step except for the occasional
snap crackle of loose gravel under her feet

Straight was her back...steady was her stride
even though she was bent and broken in spirit

Her scarred hands,
Palms and fingertips were calloused from years of using the three inch crab knife

Her heart was hardened like the shells of crabs she processed
She spoke little of her little girl times because those times were like
Dark Shadows and Days of Our Lives

Soap operas…
Days of Our Lives and Dark Shadows…with families split in loyalties of distorted love

Loving my mother, her siblings and us, her grandchildren,
At times for her was like stacked dominos

Our family life, a playing card house during the days of her life as family head

Our lives, hers, mine, ours… are forever intertwined in time's endless lines

Dorothy aka Ms. Dot

In her brokenness she stood like an oak tree planted by a river
Her spirit breathed life and died like leaves at the change of seasons
She walked tall in the hallowed halls of service to friends and foes
Forged lasting good memories in kids who knew her as Ms. Dot

Lived long enough to know the love of her son and grandsons when they were babes

Lived long enough to experience real love from a man who moved her to Tennessee

Lived long enough for peace to find her on this side of heaven

Dorothy M. Harrell-Alfred Harrell's mother

Howard C.

Tribute poem to my stepfather who died in the mid 1980s.

He stood 'bout five-foot-nine, hair speckled with black and gray
When he wasn't bent over and tired 'cause of the bricks he laid to earn his pay
From Friday night to Sunday mornin' he chased his demons away
With White Liquor and six packs of Miller
Welded to the movie screen of his brain
was the image of a man he'd killed in a Jersey bar
For a reason long forgotten like an innocent child of war
Weeknights when he wasn't drinking, we'd sit and talk
We'd sit and talk in front of the Black and White TV
While Dan Rather spewed out the evening news
I'd tell him about my newly found faith and its promise of paradise
He would tell me about how life is like a pair of dice
Sometimes you roll a seven
Other times...snake eyes
Sometimes the only the prize the winner gets
Is truth disguised as lies
He'd say, "You betta know how to shuck and jive.
Bluff your way through before you're forced to do things you never thought you'd do."
Being young and book smart dumb
I challenged his every word
Debated him down

This man with a Street University degree
This man who unselfishly made himself a father to me
His blood does not run through my veins biologically
His blood runs through my spirit energizing me mentally
When my body is tired and all my hope seems to be gone
I remember
He taught me that
It doesn't matter how strong a man is
What matters is how well
He holds on
He loved me like a son
I loved him like a Dad
To this day his voice echoes in my ears
And my heart for him, longtime dead
Still sheds a river of tears

Alfred Harrell. Dorothy M. Harrell and Howard C.

THE STATE OF BLACK

**Black People Spirituality | Blackness Speaks | Black Love
Black People Mental Health**

Black People Spirituality

History will have to record that the greatest tragedy of this period of social transition was not the strident clamor of the bad people, but the appalling silence of the good people.

- Martin Luther King, Jr.

You Cared About Me

A conversation with God

You cared about me too much to leave me where I was standing.
You gave your heart to me and I threw it back to you.
And still, Still you loved me too much to leave me where I was standing

> You loved me when I no longer loved myself.
> When I had to have it all, and you knew I'd surely fall
> I chased the world and all that it offered
> Yet still you loved me

You cared about me too much to leave me where I was standing.
You gave your heart to me, and I threw it back to you.
And still, Still you loved me too much to leave me where I was standing

> When I said, "I no longer need you," and cursed your precious name
> Planted my feet in Darkness, chose to stand in the rain
> So that the rain would hide my pain-filled tears.

You cared about me too much to leave me where I was standing.
You gave your heart to me and I threw it back to you.
And still, Still you loved me too much to leave me where I was standing

> For you see Lord, like the Prodigal son, what I had at home wasn't good
> enough.
> I- I ah-I ah had to have all that I had convinced myself was missing in my home.
> I wanted the freedom to be me.
> One cold night when I found myself sitting downtown in the cold, on a park
> bench, escaping a place, a house that wasn't a home
> I realized what I was in
> Was a place where no one cared if I lived or died.
> It was then a stranger came along and offered the warmth of his home to me.
> It was then I realized that

You care about me too much to leave me where I was standing.
You gave your heart to me.
I threw it back to you.
And still, Still you loved me too much to leave me where I was standing

BROKEN BLACK STORYTELLERS

We are humankind's healers, hope creators when all hope seems gone

We are humankind's poets, preachers, politicians, singers, songwriters,
musicians and dancers

We are time's melodies, it's rhythm of life, sang in psalms, written in proverbs,
spoken in whispers and thunder

We are Christians, Jews, Muslims, we are the builders of our world's religions

We were once united in voice to God until Nimrod started building a tower
to reach God's heaven

We are Adam's seed, created from Eden's black soil, Christ's seed created from God's
promise to Abraham

We are humankind's healers, hope creators when all hope seems gone

We are humankind's poets, preachers, politicians, singers, songwriters,
musicians and dancers

We are time's melodies, its rhythm of life, sang in psalms, written in proverbs, spoken in
whispers and thunder

We are Moses voice still speaking from the Pentateuch,
we are Jesus Christ Beatitudes proclaimers

We are Frederick Douglass' "A smile or a tear has no nationality; joy and sorrow speak
alike to all nations, and they, above all the confusion of tongues, proclaim the
brotherhood of man."

We are Langston Hughes Black Nativity
We are Maya Angelou's Caged Bird
We are Bloody Sunday in Selma
We are Black voices of salvation singing on America's holy day:

Segregated Sunday

We Are We

I am your brother, your sister, your mother, your father
I am you..you are me
We are we

Children of a lesser or greater God
We are the same, you and I, living separate joined lives
We both bleed red, die and return to Mother Earth's womb
I am you..you are me
We are we

Well at least until our heritage taught us love and hate
Taught us to love and hate each other in the names of

Religion
Race
Political affiliation
Sexual orientation

Subtly brainwashed us to believe living isn't about the "we"
Living is about "I" as if the "we" isn't the same as us
Lies craftily designed to kill the we in the "I" of us

Live In Fear...Die In Silence

When I was a younger man Fear knocked upon the door of my heart, dressed in suit and tie like a Saturday morning preacher
It preached salvation, a convincing message of paradise restoration, showed up to save my life even though it was Fear's soul, unknown to me at the time, in need of saving
My secret emotional suffering and invisible mental scars caused me to believe every word he told me caused me to exchange my private jail for his all inclusive prison of self-righteous exhalations
Like a lonely leaf raped,
Like a lonely leaf raped from a mighty oak tree by an eastern wind
I started dancing upon my winds of change
I danced...I danced
I danced until my voice surrendered its choice to speak
I danced until the muscles of my spirit grew weak and numb
It was then Fear really began his spiritual and mental manipulations with words of absolute truth, his version of life affirmations
It was then Fear clearly said, "My way is the only way you'll receive your eternal reward."
It was then Fear began creating an ongoing mental redaction of my life story, present, past, future, using the ink of time to blindfold my mind
Ink... Fear failed to realize ink eventually fades and that blindfolds fall like a well played hand of cards do to the Aces of time
In time, years far from my young adulthood, my voice rediscovered its power of choice to speak words through the freedom of putting pen to paper to...
To serve Fear divorce papers from a life I was living while slowly dying inside like a man serving a life sentence for a crime committed by his shadow
I severed all ties with Fears religious ideologies fostered in a loss of personal voice and choice
I chose to no longer live noise filled silence
Fear of living life fully
Leads to dying alone

It's Not About Religion; It's About One's Relationship

"It's not about religion; it's about one's relationship," is an expression often used by many people of the Christian faith; however, is it possible for one to exist without the other? In my opinion, it is impossible to practice one without the other. Why do I believe this way? My recent endeavors to learn more about my spiritual roots as a member of the African-American church has convinced me to accept this way of thinking and believing.

The rich spiritual history of what is known as the African-American church is saturated with both concepts and continues to be the life sustaining blood which flows through the spiritual veins of our collective African-American consciousness. The unity of relationship with strong spiritual religious practices on both the personal and communal levels continues to be the raging fire that burns from the time of our existence in slavery through the Jim Crow years in America's South into the Civil Rights Movement and now manifests its flames as the Black Lives Matter movement, Moral Mondays marches and other types of fights for our rightful places as African-Americans. Yes! Spiritually while personal and communal is for a lot of us, not all, the connective tissue to godlike presence in us even though it manifests itself in different understandings as to whether our personal belief system is about religion-denominational practices, relationship or spirituality.

The importance of a personal relationship with God, in my opinion, however one defines such, continues to be the cement that becomes the concrete us as individuals and as a community stand on. To put it as one Christian hymnal says; On Christ the Solid Rock I stand All other ground is sinking sand."

"My Hope Is Built on Nothing Less" is a Christian hymn written by Edward Mote, a pastor at Rehoboth Baptist Church in Horsham, West Sussex. Mote wrote around 100 hymns with this one, which he wrote in 1834, being his best known.
The refrain of "My Hope Is Built on Nothing Less" refers to the Parable of the Wise and the Foolish Builders and builds around the metaphor of Christ as a rock with a firm basis in Scripture (1 Corinthians 10:4).

On Christ the Solid Rock I stand

All other ground is sinking sand

"My Hope Is Built on Nothing Less" is part of the gospel hymns genre. The first stanza declare's God's grace; stanzas 2 and 3 concern the application of that grace in times of trouble. In the final stanza, Mote brings his hymn full circle with the ultimate realization of God's grace.

My Hope Is Built on Nothing Less

————

In my opinion, there is also additional biblical support for the blending of personal spiritual relationship with one's approach to God in worship. Chapter 2 of the Bible book accredited to Jesus Christ's half brother James:

17 In the same way, faith also, if it has no works, is dead,

Or *dead by its own standards being* by itself.

18 But someone

Lit *will*

may *well* say, "You have faith and I have works; show me your faith without the

works, and I will show you my faith by my works."

Also,

20 But are you willing to acknowledge, you foolish person, that faith without works

is useless?

21 Was our father Abraham not justified by works when he offered up his son Isaac

on the altar? 22 You see that faith was working with his works, and

Or *by the deeds*

as a result of the works, faith was

Or *completed*

perfected;

23 and the Scripture was fulfilled which says, "And Abraham believed God, and it

was credited to him as righteousness," and he was called a friend of God.

24 You see that a person is justified by works and not by faith alone.

And as a final point to think about as to relationship and religion as it relates to our

Christian identity.

26 For just as the body without *the* spirit is dead, so also faith without works is dead.

NEW AMERICAN STANDARD BIBLE® NASB

Blackness Speaks

We are Black Men

We are Black
We are fathers
We are husbands
We are human potters
We are sons
We are not media stereotypes
We are not a lost generation
We are Black
We are Black Men

Night Angels

Into the darkness the night angels born of men
rise and fall like shooting stars traversing the vast open range of heaven

Their tails of light glowing crystallized vapors of water glow
like the light of fireflies at the turning of dusk to dark

As they reach for the fingertips of GOD

Vanishing

Like in the days of Frederick Douglas
wounds of racism continue to permeate America's soul
      Like in the days of Martin, Medgar and Malcolm
      injustice flows through America's consciousness
            Like in the days of the Civil Rights Movement
            militarized police still pounce upon peaceful protesters

Wounds of injustice shout loudly
like cracks of thunder before a summer rain storm
      Words of media paid hate-mongers
      fuel fabricated fears forcing tolerance into an unmarked grave
            Wounds of children shot upon playgrounds
            turned into battlefields bleed into cracks of asphalt
                  Words of hope drown
                  in a cesspool of failed government policies

It is our Black children that are dying vanishing like raindrops touching hot black asphalt
It is our Black children that are dying at the hands of police officers trained in the art of
war
It is our Black children that are dying and being gunned down by the god named:

      Stand Your Ground

It is our children lives that are vanishing like smoke in the wind
It is our children lives that are being played like pawns in the chess game of media
ratings

It is their blood now dripping out of Lady Justices scales that fuels the fires of peaceful
protests in the land of the free and home of the brave

It is their blood
It is our time

It is our voices that will no longer vanish like dust in the wind

Defiant Voices

Armed to the hip our country
Parents bear the broken bleeding bodies of their children in their arms
Politicians pass blame like they pass useless laws
Laws filled with loop holes while bullets pierce the air
Punching holes in innocent souls
Religious leaders preach funerals filled with empty ideologies
Such as "God needed another angel"
Such as "it was God's will"
Something has to be done since Lady Justice only cries
Wields her sword and balances her scales
When children who look like her dies
Her blindfold barely rises to crimes against Black people
Her swords swings swiftly when it is her kind
Her scales find balance when children who look like her bleed

     Defiant voices must rise
     Defiant voices must rise
     Defiant voices must rise

Lead a social revolution that blows winds of lasting change
Defiant voices must unlock the mental chains of our nation
Our nation that spends more on war than education

     Defiant voices must rise
     Defiant voices must rise
     Defiant voices must rise

Until Lady Justice's blindfold is sandblasted
Until her eyes weep an ocean of tears
Until her sword brings justice like a vigilante blade
Until her scales are finally balanced
By the raining teardrops of all loving fathers and mothers

Parental Cries

Dark nights rise over human skies
Desperate sacrificial offerings are placed at Lady Justice's feet
Demanding reasonable solutions

Before
Death of the apocalypse

Touches another college campus: remember Virginia Tech
Touches another school: dines at another Columbine and Newton Grove
Touches another movie night: Colorado… Dark Knight Rises
Touches another hooded teens life

When a Paul Blart mall cop wannabe brings a gun to a rock fight
When will enough be enough
When will we realize all bleed
When bullets dance through the air leaving holes in the innocent

Preachers, psychologists and politicians offer us sugar filled placebos
Sweets craftily designed to push us into a diabetic coma
So that we will momentarily lose consciousness
Slip into dreams served up by the Sandman
Soon to be shredded apart by the Boogieman's nightmares

Dark nights rise over human skies
Distraught parents cry
Drop tears upon the altars of unfulfilled dreams

Cry out to GOD
Cry out for understanding as to "why"
Cry out until the wells of their eyes are dry

Parental cries fall like rain from human skies
Parental cries scream for a new social revolution
Parental cries respect the right to bear arms

Problem is
Armed to the hip our nation has become
Problem is
Buying a gun is easier than buying Sudafed
Problem is
Preachers and politicians promote fear
Problems is
People do not rise from the dead like in a video game

Truth is
When victim and villain dies
Another
Parent cries

The Blindfold Fails To Fall

Lady Liberty holds Lady Justice in a chokehold
Lady Liberty says out loud "I can't breathe"
Breathless she lays limp on hot stove concrete sidewalk
Death of the Apocalypse claims her soul
Americans cry
Black Americans cry
Mexican Americans cry
White Americans cry
Hispanic Americans cry
Jewish Americans cry
Arab Americans cry
A nation of immigrants cry for justice
And another Grand Jury fails to indite
Another justified killing it determines
And the blindfold fails to fall from Lady Justice's eyes

Cancel Culture

Tell me why you love my Blackness but want to cancel my culture
Continue rewriting American history as if America's history isn't Black history
Tell me why you love my Blackness and choose to date or marry my children
Stand silent viewing chalk lines drawn around their police murdered bodies
Tell me why you love my Blackness while gentrifying my neighborhoods
Your selective memory blinds you to that without Blackness we wouldn't have stars

Black Love

She's a strong cup of black coffee in a world that is drunk on the cheap wine of shallow love.

~ https://quotelicious.com/black-love-quotes/ #quotable

Don't ever think I feel for you, or feel over you. I didn't fall in love, I rose in it.

~Toni Morrison

Letter To Karen

Dearest Karen aka Brown Skin Girl,

As we have entered your birthday season for the first time together as a couple and turned the corner on the first year on the type of relationship we had yearned for in previous times, I say happy birthday and thank you being my best friend, confidant, lover and agreeing to become my wife at some future time.

The mystical poet Rumi once wrote,"In your light I learn how to love. In your beauty, how to make poems. You dance inside my chest where no-one sees you, but sometimes I do, and that sight becomes this art." — Rumi

You are the words, living words, of that poet to me and my hearts in alignment with the rhythm of you.

Happy birthday my brown skin girl,

~Alfred Harrell

Seven Days

In seven days I have come to love you like the sun loves the moon
In seven days I have come to be the stars of your dark night
In seven days I have heard you speak your words with my breath
In seven days I have experienced that letting go is love's secret glue
In seven days we have been bond together like fire: oxygen,heat and fuel
In seven days we have experienced love like a rising Phoenix
In seven days we have embraced the possibilities of us like an ocean's tide
In seven days we have become the rising tides of love hoped for... often denied
In seven days I have seen the you of me
In seven days you have seen the me of you
In seven days you and I have discovered the we of us
In seven days...

You

You dance with me in my dreams.
You walk alongside me like the rhythm of ocean waves.
You are the soul in my spirit like the sun in a lunar eclipse.
You are the melody of my natural world's love song.

She

With the start of each morning she was his first last kiss
She said she had never experienced a love like this
Organic, simple sampled from some of life's greatest love stories
He breathed her like she was his last breath
She kissed the heart of his soul
His soul birthed in pain
Her soul kissed his spirit
His spirit intentionally now experiencing love's peace
Love's peace through her kisses
Not pieces of love like he had known in his past

Sunrise

She told him that she desired to see the sun awaken and rise, shine its smile in the Carolina blue sky while its reflection danced upon rippling waters

So he woke her up early while the stars were receiving their final kisses from the moon, had her pack a bag quickly for a trip to a moment that would eventually become a moment trapped in time

They traveled the sleeping interstate, slipped into a conversation, a conversation mixed together with prayer and dreams of forever together like the black rich soil of their love

The fog of night slowly vanished leaving wet kisses upon the eastern North Carolina fields they passed as they traveled to where she..,where she would see

Where she would see the sun awaken…rise...see its reflection dance upon the rippling waters of the Neuse river, they would stand

Stand, Embrace
Embrace each other while the Carolina blue sky embraced the sun

Karen's sunrise

Brown Skin Girl

He nicknamed her brown skin girl because of her milk chocolate skin hue and the ways her words melted away painful memories in his mental vortex faster than the milk chocolate of M & M's candy pieces melts in our mouths

30 Seconds

Thirty seconds one half of a minute meaningful moments
requesting Gods engagement in our ongoing love story

       Our love story created yes crafted daily by the fire and water of life
       Living thriving like rose bushes planted in rich soil
       Our Black love drenched in the rain water of thirty seconds of prayer

Thirty seconds one half of a minute meaningful moments
requesting Gods engagement in our ongoing love story

Living Diamond

Daughter of earth
Beautiful in earth tones
Black like coal
Beautiful in all of earth hues
Shades of sand and topsoil
Shapely thin to curvaceous
Simply gorgeous
Daughter of earth
Coal pressurized
Cooled by earthly wind
Heated by life's fire
Held by angels
Loved by men
Loved by gods
Daughter of earth
Living diamond

Heaven

The night time sky kissed the stars
The moon caressed the sun
Lovers with arms locked forever by time

She-He-They

She became more of him with each word he spoke
He became more of her with each touch of hers
They became more of each other with each breath they shared

If Love Was A Rosebush

If love was a rosebush it would be covered with drops of blood from fingers pricked by someone in search of the perfect flowers to be given an imperfect lover who believed that love is as it is in fairytales

Black People Mental Health

This section of poems includes a few mental health resources for people of color who are willing to take the necessary steps as I, the author of this book, have done to live a fuller and richer life each day.

My African-American brothers and sisters who like myself whose mental health challenges are the product of childhood trauma, I suggest adding to your library the book THINK UNBROKEN Understanding and Overcoming Childhood Trauma by Michael Anthony published by Think Unbroken Book Publishing 2019.

See appendix for mental health resources for African-Americans.

Invisible Girl

This poem is a tribute to all girls and women who fail to see their true beauty

She danced with her silhouette in the shadows of her past
She squeezed her teeny waist with her anorexic frail fingers
She forced barely digested tiny morsels from her stomachs cavern
Starved for the beauty she possessed as a little girl
She dove like a deep sea diver into translucent waters of personal disgust
She slowly became invisible
So she once again could be beautiful

One Shot One Kill

The little girl in this narrative is a fictional composite and based upon stories of molestation that have been shared with me in confidentiality

Mommy he touches me...mommy he touches me...mommy...mommy...mommy
I know baby. He has to to tuck you in bed when I'm working late and not here
No mommy!...No mommy...I mean..
You mean he touches you during bedtime stories so you'll sleep

No mommy... no mommy...no mommy...No!

He holds my legs open...see mommy see...see mommy see...
My blood on my sheets

Oh baby! You're growing up so fast...you've had your first period like a woman
No mommy...no mommy...no mommy...No!
I was your world before you became his girl
No mommy...no mommy...no mommy...No!
Please mommy...please...believe me

Patty's repetitive stories about her private place being played with
Pushed her mommy into deeper depths of denial
Pushed Patty to pickup a gun and exit her living hell

One shot

One kill

Her Masters

Periodically as a child she danced upon her step-dads lap
Pressed up and down her innocent frame to his twisted commands
As he whispered them quietly into her tiny ears
As an adult she went to college
Earned a Masters degree in Creative Writing
Started penning her life story in poetry and prose
Stroking paper with pen until the ink bled like her first... period
She told her story for it was a generational one
She wrote poetic narratives that ejaculated forbidden words
She mastered her work of words written in her own flesh and blood

Five

I was only 5 when you left us behind in the hands of a troubled mind
My sister was just 3 when she became something a little girl should never be
We were just kids when you left us behind in the hands of a troubled mind
Our mom protected us the best she could after you packed your bags and ran
After all these years I finally get it: you were just a guy with a penis trying to be a man
You could have been our savior from mom's mom loving us like her special flavor
I was only 5, a little boy locked behind a wooden door listening to sounds
Listening to the sounds of my sister being rocked in a bedroom with a squeaky floor
I was only 5...my sister only 3 when you left us behind
Left us behind in the hands of a troubled mind

I Am My Grandmother's Son

I watched her whitewash words like she washed clothes with a washing board
We didn't have a washing machine, that was something rich folk and white folk had
I watched her cook and clean up messes of unspoken sins of selfish gratification

We,
tiny children, my sister and I, walked the streets of town, didn't have a car like aunt Viola
I listened to her speak words of love laced with Ex Lax, bitter sweet, pleasant to tongue
Tantalizing until it gave you the shits

I watched
I listened
I learned
I am my grandmother's son
The word wizard
The lover
The manipulator
The guardian
The angel
The demon
The man
The little boy lost
The man-child

The Man-child

"I exhort you also to take part in the great combat, which is the combat of life, and greater than every other earthly conflict."

~ Plato

He was yet he was not
Putting pen to paper he wrote poetry and prose
He was yet he was not
Like thunder before torrential rains
He was yet he was not
Physically visible and invisible like the god he prayed to
"Now I lay me to sleep, I pray the Lord my soul to keep
If I should die before I wake, I pray the Lord my soul to take"
He was yet he was not
A soul can't be taken if it's one of the living dead
He was yet he was not
His mind filled itself with mental images like flashes of lightning
He was yet he was not
His mind bent his memories like light through a prism
He was yet he was not
In transition from child to teen to man
He was yet he was not
He became a child trapped by Father time inside a man
He was yet he was not
He was a survivor like a former prisoner of war with PTSD
He was yet he was not
He told his story, he told others stories with poetry and prose
He was yet he was not...because
The living won't tell his story and the dead ain't talking
He is just another living dead man walking

Reflections

This poem was written by me, Alfred Harrell, in 2013 three years before the Batman v Superman: Dawn of Justice movie was released.

I was their hero until I got shot by a Kryptonite bullet

Killed

I was like Superman because even a man of steel can bleed
I was their hero until The Joker's attacks night after night
Finally forcing me to choose
Which life I would save
Which life I would lose

It was then my face of innocence began to resemble one of madness
It was then crazed and confused I rode off into the rain like the Dark Knight
It was then I rode off alone through my nighttime thunderstorms

It was then, now fallen from Heaven to Hell, I cried out like Lazarus to God
It was then, I called out to God for their salvation, not my own
It was then I became like the man who denied me his nameThe father I've never known

It was now I became just a man...a man totally broken like the Dark Knight
It was now I finally lost the battle within
It was now Heaven revealed the tears I was never allowed to cry
It was now I became a man with blood stained hands

It was now my battle damaged costume of customized skin
Revealed the darkness of my soul
It was then the fear I had hidden from family and friends swept me into its abyss
It was then fear of being a solitary image wrapped itself around my heart

It was now I had nothing to live for and even less to die for
It was now I looked at my reflection in my life's cracked up mirror
It was now I wasn't sure if I was their hero or a coward pretending to be one

It was now I realized all I was
Was a man in a costume of customized skin that hid the hero, And
And the scared little boy within

LOVE A TWISTED TROUBLED SOUL

Date: May 14, 2022 On this day they buried my biological sister, she was another mental abuser of mine from her teen years through adult life this poem is about her and the worst of traits that she shared with our maternal grandmother. May her soul finally have peace.

If love was a twisted troubled soul
     she would be our grandmother's twin sister
         living one life in reality, the other The Twilight Zone.
That is if love could be a twisted soul.

The poem following this information is tribute to the men who never survive such abuse however it could also apply to any gender involved in abusive relationship.

Information About Domestic Violence

According to the National Coalition Against Domestic Violence website, these are the statistics for men in abusive relationships.

1 in 4 women and 1 in 9 men experience severe intimate partner physical violence, intimate partner contact sexual violence, and/or intimate partner stalking with impacts such as injury, fearfulness, post-traumatic stress disorder, use of victim services, contraction of sexually transmitted diseases, etc.

1 in 3 women and 1 in 4 men have experienced some form of physical violence by an intimate partner. This includes a range of behaviors (e.g. slapping, shoving, pushing) and in some cases might not be considered "domestic violence."

1 in 7 women and 1 in 25 men have been injured by an intimate partner.

Why

The steel wire brush left linear lines upon his skin turned into a canvas
Red streaks flowed from his pores like water mixed with blood from Christ side
Beheaded was his soul by the words of the broken doll he loved more than life
His final chest compression silently asked, "Why?"

Why was he no longer her sculpture ...David
        A marble stone image of a son of a god

Why had he now become like the artwork of one of Charles Manson's disciples
Why he wondered as he slowly died
Why had he become her living canvas

Why

INTRODUCTION TO PERCH

Alfred has spoken now I will speak…
My name is Perch…

According to what I was told by Ms. Delzora, the lady who raised me from my infancy, I was buried alive after my birth in a tree covered field between a fence made of scrap lumber and a holy place. My bloodline grandmother left my tiny body for a short while in a shallow grave and until a small piece of a conscious pricked what was left of her wounded heart caused her to retrieve me, sparing my life. This is how I ended up living with Ms. Delzora who for a better choice of words was a practitioner of Christianity blended with African spirituality.

Oh! Why did I say, Alfred has spoken and now I will speak. When I became a teenager, three things happened: Ms. Delzora told me that I had a half-brother, I was given a Christian baptism in the Pungo River per small Black church tradition and upon my exiting the water I received mental as well as spiritual clarity as to who my father was plus some unique abilities because of my fraternal bloodline. Now I will share some of my life story, an altered story that started in the small town or Safe Harbor. Safe Harbor where the innocent are sacrificed for the pleasures of the living and resurrected by children of the gods who have roamed the Earth and still do some believe as spirit-like beings manifesting themselves as humans to avenge the blood of anyone taken without just cause.

Byproduct-SHE

She was lying there smelling like sex and burnt cigarettes when I arrived. Her eyes were wide open, pale white in color like the pale colored white dried cum that covered the insides of her black,African-American, thighs. She was collateral damage of a sexual encounter gone wrong. She was the byproduct of a bad fuck!

In the hearts of the living, she was shit out of luck as she laid there upon the blood stained sheets, separated from life like a moonless night is separated from the sun filled sky.
Being one once buried and left for dead like the Christ crucified I was now her only hope for justice and life denied; that which breathed life into me, I would now use to breathe life into her.

With a kiss upon her now stiffening lips I, Perch, breathed new life into her cold soul like the wind breathes life into oceans waves.
With the language of gods I spoke resurrection into her right ear.
The same ear that earlier heard, before she took her last breath," Die bitch!

Spirit Ties

"The first man, Adam, became a living person." But the last Adam—that is, Christ—is a life-giving Spirit.

~1 Cor. 15:45

Two lives, one womb, birthed years apart, connected to each other like Christ and Adam however their lives is not a biblical narrative with a prophetic ending.
Two lives bond in a spirit tie, blessed and cursed by a God who blessed them to live when they should have died.
Two lives.
One spirit tie.

….the story of Perch to be continued

Appendix

Mental health resources for African-Americans recommended by the National Alliance on Mental Illness

~ NAMI Black/African American

Your Journey

What happens at the intersection of mental health and one's experience as a member of the Black community? While the experience of being Black in America varies tremendously, there are shared cultural factors that play a role in helping define mental health and supporting well-being, resiliency and healing.

Part of this shared cultural experience — family connections, values, expression through spirituality or music, reliance on community and religious networks — are enriching and can be great sources of strength and support.

However, another part of this shared experience is facing racism, discrimination and inequity that can significantly affect a person's mental health. Being treated or perceived as "less than" because of the color of your skin can be stressful and even traumatizing. Additionally, members of the Black community face structural challenges accessing the care and treatment they need.

According to the Health and Human Services Office of Minority Health, Black adults in the U.S. are more likely than white adults to report persistent symptoms of emotional distress, such as sadness, hopelessness and feeling like everything is an effort. Black adults living below the poverty line are more than twice as likely to report serious psychological distress than those with more financial security.

Despite the needs, only one in three Black adults who need mental health care receive it. According to the American Psychiatric Association's Mental Health Facts for African Americans guide, they are also:

- Less likely to receive guideline-consistent care
- Less frequently included in research
- More likely to use emergency rooms or primary care (rather than mental health specialists)

Barriers To Mental Health Care

Socioeconomic Disparities

Socioeconomic factors can make treatment options less available. In 2018, 11.5% of Black adults in the U.S. had no form of health insurance.

The Black community, like other communities of color, are more likely to experience socioeconomic disparities such as exclusion from health, educational, social and economic resources. These disparities may contribute to worse mental health outcomes.

Stigma

Negative attitudes and beliefs towards people who live with mental health conditions is pervasive within the U.S. and can be particularly strong within the Black community. One study showed that 63% of Black people believe that a mental health condition is a sign of personal weakness. As a result, people may experience shame about having a mental illness and worry that they may be discriminated against due to their condition.

For many in the Black community, it can be incredibly challenging to discuss the topic of mental health due to this concern about how they may be perceived by others. This fear could prevent people from seeking mental health care when they really need it.

Additionally, many people choose to seek support from their faith community rather than seeking a medical diagnosis. In many Black communities in the U.S., the church, mosque or other faith institution can play a central role as a meeting place and source of strength.

Faith and spirituality can help in the recovery process and be an important part of a treatment plan. For example, spiritual leaders and faith communities can provide support and reduce isolation. However, they should not be the *only* option for people whose daily functioning is impaired by mental health symptoms.

Provider Bias and Inequality of Care

Black people have historically been negatively affected by prejudice and discrimination in the health care system in the US. And, unfortunately, many Black people *still* have these negative experiences when they attempt to seek treatment. Provider bias, both conscious and unconscious, and a lack of cultural competency can result in misdiagnosis and inadequate treatment. This ultimately can lead to mistrust of mental health professionals and create a barrier for many to engage in treatment.

Black people may also be more likely to identify and describe physical symptoms related to mental health problems. For example, they may describe bodily aches and pains when talking about depression. A health care provider who is not culturally competent might not recognize these as symptoms of a mental health condition. Additionally, Black men are more likely to receive a misdiagnosis of schizophrenia when expressing symptoms related to mood disorders or PTSD.

How To Seek Culturally Competent Care

When a person is experiencing challenges with their mental health, it is essential for them to receive quality care as soon as the symptoms are recognized. It is equally important that the care they receive is provided by culturally competent health care professionals.

While we recommend seeking help from a mental health professional, a primary care professional is also a great place to start. A primary care professional might be able to provide an initial mental health assessment and referral to a mental health professional if needed. Community and faith organizations may also have a list of available mental health providers in your area.

When meeting with a provider, it can be helpful to ask questions to get a sense of their level of cultural awareness. Providers expect and welcome questions from their patients or clients, since this helps them better understand what is important in their treatment. Here are some sample questions:

- Have you treated other Black people or received training in cultural competence for Black mental health? If not, how do you plan to provide me with culturally sensitive, patient-centered care?
- How do you see our cultural backgrounds influencing our communication and my treatment?
- Do you use a different approach in your treatment when working with patients from different cultural backgrounds?
- What is your current understanding of differences in health outcomes for Black patients?

Whether you seek help from a primary care professional or a mental health professional, you should finish your sessions with the health care professional feeling heard and respected. You may want to ask yourself:

- Did my provider communicate effectively with me?
- Is my provider willing to integrate my beliefs, practices, identity and cultural background into my treatment plan?
- Did I feel like I was treated with respect and dignity?
- Do I feel like my provider understands and relates well with me?

The relationship and communication between a person and their mental health provider is a key aspect of treatment. It's very important for a person to feel that their identity is understood by their provider in order to receive the best possible support and care.

More Information

If finances are preventing you from finding help, contact a local health or mental health clinic or your local government to see what services you qualify for. You can find contact information online at findtreatment.samhsa.gov or by calling the National Treatment Referral Helpline at 800-662-HELP (4357).

NAMI's Sharing Hope Program

Sharing Hope is a one-hour program to increase mental health awareness in Black communities by sharing the presenters' journeys to recovery and exploring signs and symptoms of mental health conditions. The program also highlights how to navigate the mental health system.

"Sharing Hope: An African American Guide to Mental Health" provides mental health information in a sensitive manner through personal stories. Recovery is possible, and this booklet tells you where to find more information, seek help and be supportive. You can buy hard copies through the NAMI Bookstore.

Black Mental Health Resources

Please note: The resources included here are not endorsed by NAMI, and NAMI is not responsible for the content of or service provided by any of these resources.

Black Emotional and Mental Health Collective (BEAM)

Group aimed at removing the barriers that Black people experience getting access to or staying connected with emotional health care and healing. They do this through education, training, advocacy and the creative arts.

Black Men Heal

Limited and selective free mental health service opportunities for Black men.

Black Mental Health Alliance — (410) 338-2642

Provides information and resources and a "Find a Therapist" locator to connect with a culturally competent mental health professional.

Black Mental Wellness

Provides access to evidence-based information and resources about mental health and behavioral health topics from a Black perspective, as well as training opportunities for students and professionals.

Black Women's Health Imperative

Organization advancing health equity and social justice for Black women through policy, advocacy, education, research and leadership development.

Boris Lawrence Henson Foundation

BLHF has launched the COVID-19 Free Virtual Therapy Support Campaign to raise money for mental health services provided by licensed clinicians in our network. Individuals with life-changing stressors and anxiety related to the coronavirus will have the cost for up to five (5) individual sessions defrayed on a first come, first serve basis until all funds are committed or exhausted.

Brother You're on My Mind

An initiative launched by Omega Psi Phi Fraternity, Inc. and NIMHD to raise awareness of the mental health challenges associated with depression and stress that affect Black men and families. Website offers an online *toolkit that provides Omega Psi Phi Fraternity chapters with the materials needed to educate fellow fraternity brothers and community members on depression and stress in Black men.*

Ebony's Mental Health Resources by State

List of Black-owned and focused mental health resources by state as compiled by Ebony magazine.

Hurdle

Provides culturally sensitive self-care support and teletherapy for Black men and their families. Currently in pilot program available only to residents of MD, VA and DC. Residents of other states can join their waiting list and will be notified when Hurdle is available in their state.

Melanin and Mental Health

Connects individuals with culturally competent clinicians committed to serving the mental health needs of Black & Latinx/Hispanic communities. Promotes the growth and healing of diverse communities through its website, online directory and events.

Ourselves Black

Provides information on promoting mental health and developing positive coping mechanisms through a podcast, online magazine and online discussion groups.

POC Online Classroom

Contains readings on the importance of self care, mental health care, and healing for people of color and within activist movements.

Sista Afya

Organization that provides mental wellness education, resource connection and community support for Black women.

Therapy for Black Girls

Online space dedicated to encouraging the mental wellness of Black women and girls. Offers listing of mental health professionals across the country who provide high quality, culturally competent services to Black women and girls, an informational podcast and an online support community.

The SIWE Project

Non-profit dedicated to promoting mental health awareness throughout the global Black community.

The Steve Fund

Organization focused on supporting the mental health and emotional well-being of young people of color.

Unapologetically Us

Online community for Black women to seek support.

NAMI
4301 Wilson Blvd. Suite 300
Arlington, VA 22203
Helpline: 800-950-6264
In Crisis text: NAMI to 741741
Member Services 888-999-6264

Mental Health Statics and Resources for African-Americans from NAMI National Alliance on Mental Illness. Shared from its website:
www.nami.org/Your Journoy/Idontity-and-Cultural-Dimensions/Black-African-American